momently

Momently

Zach Savich

Black Ocean
Boston · Chicago

Black Ocean
P.O. Box 52030
Boston, MA 02205
blackocean.org

ISBN: 978-1-939568-77-9

Library of Congress Control Number: 2024930071

Printed in Canada

FIRST EDITION

To HP & AP & JC

CONTENTS

garden party

the suits we made to endure the unendurable fire   could not   so we
made them   prettier and we made them   for longer   feathers and
fur in barbed wire do not soften it

I bend the barbed wire true   I balance the nail in a hole already in
the wall   I cook on low to heat the house   snow worn in the path to
the woodpile   flowers first   in the path to the woodpile

foal is a color   there is no restoration only rest for what is

the compass needle refines until   precision blurs   who would blame
fern armor   who would blame a cardboard harmonica   to say it and
it won't become information

ethics meaning   don't summarize   here is a birdhouse here is a
birdhouse for no bird here is a birdhouse for no bird that has ever
before felt at home enough to appear

a question is understanding a question   is saying yes   the circuit
burns out as soon as it fires   it can fire for a while though

patio hammer

left the ladder in saplings   a decade later I saw it   between the music
aloft   do you like this music   I like music   leaving your house even
the cut grass smelled of basil

rainwater in the rooftarp   it's not for drinking   built the chimney
around the tree   like that you said like what   just all of it   lightning
broke the angel's trumpet off at the wrist   the mouth appears singing

and death was a house   a little bee   could hide with one wing   or one
ant in a vein

alive for a minute a long long minute

I water the fire escape garden with a mug   shoebox roses in ashes
sawdust bridges   stone boats   patience rests in a debt of tissue stems
bullet-small winds we are due

or did you see the following finch first   or was another farther behind
and how far is still   pursuit or perhaps   now orbit

we'll have more years ahead some other year   how did you sleep did
you sleep   more of what there is nothing like is what I like   precise as
light in a pepsi can

driveway globe

the conditions you need to think about the most make it impossible
have I loved it enough for it to be enough   here   where not even ruin
lasts

an ethics of deciding to see   considered meeting you at the station but
remembered the pleasure of finding another's home in its instances the
music not cued but playing   the rain of blood was dung from passing
butterflies

forgot to send you the book read it myself again   as in a late sonata not
more beautiful for being late but late and more beautiful   and peace was
a wind from far through the house   the curtains would move from it
but to it the windows are bare

pears

the less water the stronger the mortar   the lower the frequency the
farther sound travels   a sharp blade won't reflect light   lives have been
changed by less

it's the language you can stand when you can't stand language   dented
a/c on a sill   totaled windstar   in dandelion stems   cheerios on a
trampoline   the construction goes on forever   we sleep between
hammers

or there's the late mannerism   of groundling leaves drawing bees
they hem the hues   no profit in it   if profit is eventual honey

megachurch

there's little difference between saying what you believe and saying what
you hope could have an effect you could believe in   dust rises and you
can cover your mouth or eyes

or to pause as though on a dirt track   in an unintended alley   where
birds   gather haircut scraps into · we suppose   nests   gathering
sometimes into flight or a glimpse or as though   on a dirt track rutted
and mended with leaves   stay on the leaves   do not trouble their
mending

or finding you at the upstairs sink   tending a stain   or just finding
you there   innuendo of shirt softer than steam   apples peaches pears
on a single bough

muster

as there are some things the wind puts right   as wind is one   as
needle-petaled yellow blossoms line the sill   here is a wine from
grapes grown only in blizzard   serve it warm

let the preamble continue   let the poem be harder and happy   oh
poetry help us understand less much better   catalpa breeze   a
driveway recital   7 child cellists just outside

knife cleaned by its fruit   it had to happen to stop happening   if
the fantasy is continuing

lute berry

put a petal on the nail   press my hand sharp   another petal on the nail
press my hand sharp   another petal on the nail   press sharp   until
petals compound to cushion the spike   now make a headband exactly
that thickness of petals

being time's interlude we start each prayer *at least*   I want what's so
honest it can't be said looking in another's eyes   not even noon in the
janky birdbath   and the water as warm as it will be

the meaning that means the most hasn't yet   hose left running washing
half-dug stump roots   hosing the ginkgo leaves   refrigerator box of a
whole tree's leaves   coming apart so it holds more   but holds together
less

entropy multiples coincidence   or to have been ruined *for*   in the
immense gentling sense

today the third graders are learning impermanence   by dumping ash
portraits of their parents   into the river   portraits made ash by ash
in the bottom of shoeboxes·   the quiz asks   where are your parents
now   where is the river   are you wearing the shoebox's shoes

more ripeness in *fresh fruit* on the hand-painted sign   you make what you
want to see then see more like it   fruit injured before ripening   then
injured and ripe

though sadly a faith in entropy only gets you so far   because some things
do last   at least so far as we do   it startles the blur in its woodsy hue
forgetting is all right if you keep remembering or forgetting fast enough

now we move to the plane the firefighters burn each spring   I fix the
spring in the wrench

during the flood they loaded the library into vans sedans crates on a bike
after the flood the catalog said to find this novel find this house on
bradford road   read inside   on a piano bench with music inside
ambulette   a little walk   little ambulance

hymn

is it better to be past but not yet beyond   or beyond but not yet past   I
work on the thing until it's too ruined to work   I tie a stone around
my neck and leave the river

I tie a string around each stem   I don't need to begin others have   I
start with their beginnings remember them a bit   delible   I resolved
to take care of mountains whatever that means

magnolias preceded bees   evolved to be pollinated by beetles   evolved
hardy blossoms to endure it

silo grey

what evidence has the world provided   of what   of the world
providing

the fireplace should be as wide in inches as the wall in feet   put rubble
in the wall as you go   it devastates   and insulates

children   selling boughs at the peak   to cyclists without brakes
dragging behind to slow   they come apart like sparks   sprinkler on
in rain   radio in a stroller   I tire finely   or is one bird with two
stones better than one with one or two with three   or than finding
one bird   or two stones   on a threshold

taping the windows

style deviates   it countenances more, than precision   in our last
argument I said he should revise everything into a single line   I should
have said this line can be as long as you can   as water returned to the
farthest well

ribbons where the trail will be ribbons in my hair   to stay forever on a
brink   to be forever's brink   as the stoic moment a berry knows when
you pull it   easy   off a stem   as the body weeps to consume   loose-
knit for the spring wind

do you remember not learning to count but to determine a rhythm   so
to be by a rhythm   determined   it could still happen once or twice
in the afternoon a shower   the coffee cools so we chill it   evening's
coffee   it banters nice and so on

the adult longeing guide

tell yourself it will be a season even though it will be a year   tell yourself
it will be a year   as the music   which is downstairs   leaves forever a
portion   which may be altogether how small

longeing pronounced *lunging*   a term for exercising a horse on a line
forgery concealed   in a painting in earnest   intensified is lasting in its
way   for a finale the orchestra tunes

the winner is   congratulations

equivalent to murals

let the middle be composed by another   I swerve to avoid apples in
the road   children in the mirror adjust the apples   so the next driver
can't miss

it's only indispensable like boats on a busted reservoir   or formal dances
in improvised films   one arrives instead   for how long   oh just
forever   does not the fruit last longer than the seeds   in my mouth
yes

trucks on blocks long past tinkering   you paint where you can reach
how's his color today   he has color enough   a fox   thrums
the gravel brink   I watch until I hear   *thrums the gravel brink*   isn't it
darling   like a stilt dancer rambunctious in mud

cold lamp

it was the morning desire first distinguishes itself from and then for the
beloved   it was the season everybody paints houses blue   for a blue
home   if the light is yellow   paint green

which touched me like   is this the piano or the outside of the piano
then   *this is the piano*   playing a chord

I trust most the prophets who hesitant ask *is that a prophet*   prophet-
shadow of a sparrow on the prophet-shadow of a branch   that's nest
enough

branch through the window

for so long wishing to end   let the weight of the axe do the work   and
if there is no axe   let the weight of the air   and if there is no air   let
the weight of the air

who would blame a paper axe   who would blame twine wires   travel
taught me to disappear in place   when you don't know enough to
decide you decide

each broken part lasts longer   oh break it more   decadent as a glass
of ice or a bicycle for summer   leave it on a dune   you can pour
what's left into the vase   inestimable prettiness of hinges more perma-
nent than doors   cathedral built with a battered door

smithereens

the durable fantasy isn't of durability   but duration   leaves too small
to rake   loving air through the door so much I forget to go out

transcendence is pedestrian   I saw a caterpillar gone to translucent
lengths   the particular blue of salon posters long in a window   grass
under a boat too long on a lawn   crystal anchor

I held that a still note holds most   still the most I might hold   is what
a still note won't   and to do so   and to do so   anything starts *in
medias res* if you say it

vascular

I made the motel colder for the flowers   put my phone in the plastic
ice bucket's liner in case it's raining and I'm out in it   if you are
shell at least have ocean sound in you   bad advice   if you are shell
have shell in you

friends tell me the books you are reading   am I there   if so distract
me until I arrive   put the basil where the light is most basil

I put mesh over the rose petal jar   I don't know why   C. did it
once   never mind shining the kettle   the water shines   paint
holds the wire

featured totalities

forever is transitional   the first naturally grown human wings were
wooden wings in rain   but I'm not sure what is former grandeur
maybe a wooden wedding ring its gem   held in place by hand   a pier
from a pile   across the street a kid dumps bacon grease in the family
dollar lot

it's enough to have made peace once even for a moment   now what do
you make of that   petals and glass in gravel and moss   like snow in a
crocus flute   or valleys in gospel tunes

given the shortness of life   it's fine to act like it's longer   house
with one doorknob   move it room to room

sparkles

fruit in the borrowed home ages in places selected for aesthetics   peach
deep in an orange vase   cherries on the dictionary mark my word   it
isn't music it helps you hear it

the match burns down and you shake the burn from your hand   what
animal will that call   as every coincidence confides   pulling my hair
to add to the broom

my fortune was the tea bag broke   I drank the leaves   what poetry
means to me is reading a poem   looking up *pinning down* I found *pinion*
is on the wing   it's not a central feather   it's central to flying   a
butterfly probably rode on one one time   I wanted that riding   I
wanted that riding to leave me   I wanted that riding to leave me bereft
beset freshest and worn

sinew

not remembering is one way for memory to not be a problem   if you
can remember that   I stop the bleeding by leaning back   what barely
coheres testifies most to coherence   mow two days before the wedding
have it rain that morning

and what was the dead one's favorite song   and how long will it be
oh turn the dead's gardening gloves over in rain   let them soak even
small birds shelter in the statue's missing arm

paradise cannot counteract so it must contain (the suffering)   the
suffering paradise cannot counteract   so it must contain   if you pour
the boiling slow enough   it cools   storefront church's boombox
drowned by the choir

other dusks

D. tells us forty-five leaves is the rule of thumb for each apple   so
perfectly I am recalling marksmen winnowing additional leaves from a
bough   in the films of archery as a child   as in the films of archery as
a child   no matter how many arrows fly or how far   there are always
more in the quiver

the red-winged blackbird would be a red-winged blackbird without red
without wings   the one key on my chain   could have any name
marriage divorce neighbors lean wrought scrap on the fence hosing it clean
hosing the horizon

never closer to understanding   never farther from trying to   today's
a record a used   bookstore plays Saturdays

chandelier

what message could you see on the path to make you   stop or hurry
past   and return   the problem with most things is they're already
something else

I count slower to give everyone longer to hide   there's what no one
wants to hear and what no one hears   rowers pull alongside the river
could we turn events back into instances   all the versions of this
song are live

scant rosemary barely enough   for one bee   I knew he'd pretend he
knew any poet I mentioned   so I mentioned my friend

hurt silk

begin with a simple grammatical rule   say the hardest thing you can
then look around   you don't have to write the hardest thing down
say what you see when you turn

another game was imagine an evil intelligence will end us unless we say
x or y   with sufficient tenderness   another game was imagine we're
already ended   how can you say x or y   pardonably

the secret of the trick was   we saw it   watched a kid acrobat practice
on shadows   if you fall from a shadow   that's far

this is steam

these values permit enduring   they may not themselves endure   glycol
ether esters prevent spray paint from drying in midair   spray paint falling
snow   dew on a thorn   glistens and warns

you see what you see wrong   the cinder path is made of the partially
combusted   it could burn more   I always forget if you're allowed
to drink in the hospital   like after someone gives birth   champagne
he said   opening a beer

steam clanks back   through the same pipe   the preserved eternal
blossom   is no blossom

luna pier

harder to write myself a note   on the back of the eulogy   than the
eulogy   it takes a long time to tune   and longer to trust   sometimes
the captions say [gentle minor melody]   sometimes [wind activates the
motion alarm]

the fantasy at thirty-nine is a hamburger in the parking lot   by the squat
lighthouse   scrap beach   golf cart worn to metal   there isn't room
on the shelf so I keep reading

years I traveled with a suit in the trunk   in case of   the eventual
and a shovel for snow   I came around to regret   outlived one apple
blossom   I don't know which

proposal

I decide coffee alone will not heal me   is there sugar   I returned to
earth for coffee   I saw no need to forgive me   I had to do it and did
it nevertheless

put a seed in the empty room   rots   another seed   rots   another
seed   rots   another seed   rots   until one seed roots in the rot-new
earth   what you can bear to say is not what you can bear to have said
or repeat

cooling trunks in the abundant demolished lot   delays blossoming
cooling with a hose

heights hardware

when you imagined this house   what did you think would happen   all
you get to be is alive   a tilted trellis for ordered vines

the date of the founding was painted much later   on the brick side   the
painting much later signed   bodega roses   in their exhaustion
painterly   and spiral bound   in the heavy knit

you could do worse   than write a poem to summon wind   or to read
one   and notice wind

horizon turned like the line of the throat

according to theories of color charred matchheads (dark) absorb ambient
light   therefore heat   therefore there's more warmth in their spent
ends than in a flash   but how to feel that

in the absence or imperfection of optical instruments you could descend
a telescopic pit   look up   it has the same effect   I look up the tree
in the book   matches in a blue dish   with blue waves a blue ship
someone is diving or pulling a whale

instead of saying how you feel you say all the ways a person might   but
that's how I felt   they say the wounds from lightning are cold   oysters
hold old sun

bradford

I don't want to know what the deer see behind the shed   but what they
think might appear   an elegy for those who will survive us

you stop noticing the insects after a while   that is you stop   noticing
yourself   athletic shorts from the pharmacy   the afternoon inking
through   windows in newsprint   gaze now a horizon or is it the field
I ran for it

the pitcher unlearns his arm   a form now easy to fault   but if it ever
works   wow

good humor

advances in music technology have done nothing   for ice cream truck
music technology   it is best jangly cloying unchanged   the brakes go
and I   coast right   .

rusted water towers hold the purest water   lilies and quarry bounds
the slash grass   the soul is circumstantial   evidence of it is not   it's
like describing someone watching someone play a video game   flowers
visible just in the peripheral

I outlived regret   she was peeling a clementine behind an olive garden
cataracts and ash trees   told me about her daughter's betta fish
wondered if I'd ever seen the office

midway

bees vanish but also hive in more spots   sunglasses in grasses   a
billowing tarp   plein air evidence of their going   rust prevents
corrosion   you're trying to make a place   more than to make it to a
place   vegetal rust

wrens campari-rinsed   it serves   she said the tumors must be holy
bringing you   as they do   so close   clothesline cloudburst and clovers

the mind's more wax than wick   posts abraded soft   a psalm that starts
perhaps   perhaps try this same piece of the puzzle   in the same gap
next month

farther gardens

every coincidence confides just so   each brink becomes a brim   as
a storm that never breaks   storming all afternoon and no storm still
wind turns the page   we read from here

being past wisdom   wind enters wind so there is wind   and a blue
stone   music box with no music but gentle its key and the ballerina rises
an inch

has it been too much dying certainly   pouring wine onto the broken
bottle it means   I must have been carrying this wine in my mouth   the
world will reply I don't need to

intimates

the hardest part of the long-distance sled race is feeding the dogs   ice in the frozen meat hydrates the team

it was too hot to touch so I gripped it   displaced the heat

we had live birds you could pin in your hair   and there was a target you started very near   and every time you hit it you had to step back   and there was a target you started so far from   and any time you hit it you had to step toward   where do those paths meet today   what target is just to the side

chalk ribbon

the world will end I don't need to   pebbles around mint filter rain
mittens tied to bike handles   dry the slide with them   if the crate is too
heavy eat one of its oranges

we burn the toxins off the filing cabinet   for mushrooms or bees   to
open a door   open another door   to lift a boulder each morning
approach   to lift a robin   watch   threw a stone at the bass stuck
between rocks   how else could I free it

as the electrician ducks under the b-ball hoop exiting   his tall van   who
would blame a toothpick fusebox   if the crate is still too heavy   oh
carry it

community garden winter

this is how you keep talking to someone who's crying and cry   there was
that dog   that only children see   it's a corgi   places fire feeds on rain
colorless rainbows   passing under the dry bouquet

just ask them to stand on the stage   during the hard speech   and look
at the harp   this way of swimming works only in currents   you look
for a fact and find a phrase   children with hands too small to drink from
wading with open mouths

a kite must be one of several shapes to fly   but it may be several of them
or several that don't   as long as   at the right moment   it isn't

scrap diamond

or tell me about leaves that turn green again   or another green   and
never fall   I have written a book to press them in   we turn the heat all
the way up in case   it goes out soon   style survives

love being everything that isn't endless   there is infinity in everything
that isn't endless   after the magician's magic fails   there's this moment
when anything might be the trick   touching their face picking   hay
from a bale   we move to help them see the bale

your age in snow years is how many years you've seen it   your snow
birthday   is when how many years you've seen it   is the same   as
how many years you have left   I had a snow birthday once   it's been
snowing ever since

the pasture bridges

pearlescent tractor   to listen in tongues   tinsel interference   it's antibiotic

to them time was a kite in a bale   unquestioning fruit   or one with a lamp   beside her at the bus stop   you speak the truth   oysters for a dollar   it burns in

and surprisingly recently   inventors honestly thought oars   thus rowers could steer a hot air balloon   fired cannons to navigate by the report discarded clothes to lift   it was stained glass   all the way down   and the tin clouds   were tin from a tin flute   it's ethical to assume we will be in this moment forever

held a berry secretly

bucket with no bottom   holds anything it passes over   or to say too much as one steps   overdressed   into an unexpected summer   or to say less as an actor   older   less intent on lines   speaks not from but to a horse

each symptom is sufficient   but it's already another past   the grass uncut as soon as it's planted   pried stones from the path dumped in the lake   commemorating   don't yet know what

I understand eternity   I'm small in the same way   kid next door shouts *cannonball*   and steps into a pail

giornata

an hour isn't enough for anything   daycare with no sign   art doesn't
adapt   it's already adaptive   it's emphasis

the neighbors each had a way of pulling cases of beer   home in little
carts   when for any reason they couldn't drive   couldn't get warm so
wore   the softest   it was analogous   chewed ginger   I saw behind
my eyes and there were many apples

the ladders couldn't reach   but leaned   safe enough to rest   that
small way up   you can see   a page torn through   which is the
signature   appetite and rest are the same   and a basketball court
opaque in the greenhouse

permanently

one day I'll open this window   from the outside   I'll see a spider on
pewter   thistles and brick   in the washing machine   think how
different it was five years ago   it's that different whenever you want

I stay in the cover crop   the hay is mostly a rake and stripped wires
learn what you can fix by breaking   foundation settles so the door hangs
flush

that's no door   just a rake   sun on the handle   kleenex and emeralds
in tines   open it   and fill the truck with broadcast radishes   they
aerate the soil down   who knows for what   just some sky before snow
and a cello in a roped-shut trunk   rubber lining of the trunk for bait

postcard lullaby

crossing the fish gut bridge   our relationship was matinees   touching
while watching   *go home finish*   *call with it still on your voice*

ice not yet ice   woody leaves   long as branches   woodsmoke from
houses with plywood windows   the radio tells me the most
mispronounced word of the year   roofers scrape the roof of the roofing
store   inflatable nativity   geese leave the tree and there's no more tree

an allegory of the marsh   which I was too tired to see   so I walked
deeper into the osprey woods   trees on the shore with roots washed
bare   they're fine   then they'll fall   and be fine   a crane flaps
looks back   sunrise two hours after the official time   deals its cards
into my pizza box

wind gym

floral recovery day at the cemetery   that flower machine revving   the
hardest part of the drive was your own driveway   coming or going   or
somebody wading to the waist of the silhouette on his t-shirt

where would I go   he said the one time he left   the failure of imagination
sustained us   preferring the eventual to the eternal   preferring the
morning tomorrow   as long as we can   in lieu of everything

morning like a towel on a boxer's neck   denim   shards of cds in the
firepit   and a car on the dunes   made of two bicycles with benches and
a roof   my friend the windsurfer asked what's the most extreme thing
I've ever done   before I could answer   interrupted   *no fuck that
wind*

disco nap

stitches dissolve   stems in the pushmower   too fine for the blades
we could still come around   gnats and you should have

into this field of orange juice jugs   I'd only watch someone doing a
crossword for hours   if I could see only their face   zinnias
experience isn't skill   let the neighbors buy us curtains

explain what chocolate is   you've found a wrapper   dandelions wide as
seed   tendril the torn shirt   luster of a shed   take out the too-bright
bulbs   I guess I'll wear a little hat   out of respect for your childhood
pets

florid brick

told to turn at the church in the square   there are two churches in the
square   I show up at the meeting prepared   a blank page in a folder

the compass needle isn't stuck when you're shaking it   what are you
saving things for   the directions to the ferry began with grapefruit in the
garden   a lot on this pile wouldn't burn

it's hard to make something that lasts no more than a moment   the fire
escape built before the building   he said to pull grass from brick after
rain   knew it to the minute   but mostly we remember music   and it's
playing   we've lived on less   I don't park closest but where you'll expect
oh never mind the difference   further or farther

poems for future anniversaries

they'll be the easiest to publish   I throw a balled rag at the shed   soft
so it doesn't come down   to me it is gold

turn when you think you've gone too far   time and temperature the
same on the bank clock   there's this form fallen things find
bulletproof   dying will remember me   a dart board drawn in fluttering
crayon

got very good with a throwing form that'd get me every time a bullseye
and very kicked out   my experience couldn't be farther from memory
poem for the penultimate etc   to cook something slowest   hold it to
the body's heat

radiant failure

hot to the touch or hot from the touching   Cage said "thinking the
sounds worn out wore them out"   deterioration but also   as one wears
a costume out

you don't wash it off you wear it off   the heart finds its center elsewhere
in the heart   the key that locks the door will never open it   the love
that leads you to the city lives elsewhere   but lives   turning the pencil
as I write to sharpen it

didn't take part in the drawing lesson   skulls   the world was my skull
watched somebody clean hedges in the park   water bottle and   rag
just for that

dandelion fences

you find your vision where it finds you   it's just a job   *daylighting* brings
out the buried streams   not to change course   but be seen   beware
those looking for meaning not   for seeing

the riddle says the fire multiplies the snow   how   oh a reflection
around the pit   that carcass   I swear in the snapdragons   I ready
the heaven-mud   I saw behind my eyes and it was sheet metal and
autumn

feed the bird the hand around the seed   the rare feather in tall grass
is a rare bird in low   the livelong   beware those seeing meaning more
than motion   I hammered the nail as far as I could then massaged the
wood soft   push lower   if you touch here   below the throat   it
smells of rain

vanishingly

in every sport there is the skill that's last to go   learn it later   saplings
for the small stove   leave when there's one more to go

the sun sets through a curtain   I stayed awake on the drive   by
imagining telling you   I stayed awake on the drive   by imagining your
hand   tiring of the long view   it gets closer   first instruction
empty the stage   now empty it more

we sat at the table   snapping string beans   from a paper bag   kitchen
table   placemats   it tunes past snap   the string's ends   recall   a
bruise in a wire coop   on earth famous shadows include wind shadows
which are downwind   and windless

3 cacti in 4 jars

somebody left the radio on for the dog   no   it's Saturday   K.'s
practicing guitar   it happens once and continues   shirt drying on a
hinge of skylight

the distance is most distinct at the source   the meaning is I wanted to
see it   it helps but mostly for a duration   your car could make this
sound another month

birds that make their nests from this and that   wisp of ribbon cattail
feathers from others   birds that make themselves like that   can
they fly   I think that making themselves like that is a kind of flying

saginaw

shards of the ruined greenhouse cathedral   work up through the garden
kohlrabi   build the guitar around the humming string

moss gathers itself   this is a movie about an actor I'll never recognize
he pretends to read   pretends to stand and leave   in penitential
shallows   willows and gulls in church bells   there's a house in every
town painted to annoy the neighbors   and a house soiled before auction
to show it was ours

the history of eating in human history is mostly getting sick from things
that were fine before   integrity in the exurban plazas   these parking
lines were painted by hand   the piano was too large to discard so you
learned it

wooden paving stones

if you can have only two tools   does my hand   we don't pull through
we pull something through   the message is getting through

the technician says *stop breathing* works better than   *hold your breath*
summary of a journey   I stayed   distracted by tomatoes until
distracted by squash   is there hot water left or hot water again   clover
has too much protein for grazing

as one who rolls a hoop and   steps through   or do we move otherwise
to acquire a further primary shade   *I don't want you to have to find my
body* I said   *I can find your body* she said   poured too much to the cup
and bent to the cup

broom clean

by the time you reach the shore of answers   the shoal of answers   you
have no more questions   it has an answer   for that   mute swan
whistling swan   you have to *see* the difference   I hold the coat closed
another month

here is the party scene   dust on new ice   dust in ice   here is where a
roadside attraction should be   the gaze needs it   without   vacates to
a yard of styrofoam and toys   sled patching   garage door gap   gulls
and licorice   house smaller than the car outside

the thing no one needs becomes a site for needs that nothing serves
you speak the promise looking in the air   what was the meaning for
fallen branch in the fishing line in the branches   held and held

∂oan brook

yet of course the abyss has lichens   goats   beech copse where clovers
lie   like railtrack-flattened coins   the goats descend further into the
ravine   before tasting of the lichens   until then   I've put our name
in for a table   a miracle would be all right

nodded to the sidewalk person playing with broken glass they put it in
their pockets as I approached *I mean no harm* cutting their hands   tipped
the thin kid who comes from trees and is discreet and pumps your gas
until the owner tells him to go   stopped at the driveway lemonade
stand driving away I saw it live lemon trees on the porch   on the way
to the hospital pushed a car   on the way to the hospital carried a shelf
yawned and guy on a ladder said *don't yawn that shit's contagious and I'm
up a ladder up here*

don't see the idea see around   in the last act   the loom becomes a boat
weaving its own sail   for what flood   never better

Acknowledgments

Thank you to the editors and readers of the publications in which material from *Momently* first appeared:

A Dozen Nothing
Alligator Juniper
Burnside Review
Fonograf Editions Magazine
Gordon Square Review
Heavy Feather Review
Iowa Review
jubilat
Laurel Review
Longlong
On the Seawall
Puerto del Sol
Salt Hill
Small House Pamphlet Series
Under a Warm Green Linden
Verse Daily
Windfall Room
Yum! Lit

This book benefited from the support of the following organizations and their communities: the Vermont Studio Center, Amy Margolis and the Iowa Summer Writers' Festival, the Kacob House Foundation Residency, Sony Ton-Aime and the Chautauqua Institution, and Ann Ransford and the

Friends of Theodore Roethke in Saginaw, Michigan. Thank you, also, to my students and colleagues at the Cleveland Institute of Art and in the PhD in Creativity at the University of the Arts. And thanks to friends near and far, particularly David Bartone, Michael Loughran, Caryl Pagel, and Hilary Plum for years and years of drafts.

I'm especially grateful to Carrie Olivia Adams, Janaka Stucky, and all of Black Ocean's crew, authors, and readers for the world of which this book is a part.